EVANSTON·PUBLIC
LIBRARY

*Purchase of this library
material made possible
by a contribution
to the Fund for Excellence*

American Habitats

Prairie Animals

Connor Dayton

PowerKiDS press.

New York

Published in 2009 by The Rosen Publishing Group, Inc.
29 East 21st Street, New York, NY 10010

First Edition

Editor: Nicole Pristash
Book Design: Greg Tucker
Photo Researcher: Jessica Gerweck

Photo Credits: Cover © www.istockphoto.com; back cover, pp. 5, 7, 9, 13, 17 Shutterstock.com; p. 11 © Shin Yoshino/Getty Images; p. 15 © John Cornell/Getty Images; p. 19 © Joel Sartore/Getty Images; p. 21 © John Cancalosi/age fotostock.

Library of Congress Cataloging-in-Publication Data

Dayton, Connor.
  Prairie animals / Connor Dayton. — 1st ed.
      p. cm. — (American habitats)
  Includes index.
  ISBN 978-1-4358-2767-7 (library binding) — ISBN 978-1-4358-3196-4 (pbk.)
ISBN 978-1-4358-3202-2 (6-pack)
  1. Prairie animals—Juvenile literature. 2. Prairies—Juvenile literature. I. Title.
  QL115.3.D39 2009
  591.74'4—dc22
                                        2008037736

Manufactured in the United States of America

Contents

America's Prairie Animals

As you stand in the middle of a wide open **prairie**, you may feel that you are alone. However, you are not alone! A prairie **habitat** is filled with life. On a prairie, you can see grasshoppers, red-tailed hawks, bees, red foxes, and rabbits living among the tall grass.

The prairie habitat in the United States lies in the middle of the country. Prairies can be found from the Dakotas to Texas and from Wyoming to Indiana. Some of these states are called Great Plains states. Many kinds of animals make their homes in this flat, grassy habitat.

This is a pronghorn antelope. Pronghorns are tan, and they have white markings on their heads and necks.

Wide Open Spaces

A prairie is called grassland because grass is the main type of plant that grows there. Some of these grasses are big bluestem grass and switchgrass. When left uncut, these prairie grasses can grow as tall as an adult person! Prairies are also known for having lots of wildflowers, such as coneflowers and milkweed.

These plants supply plenty of food for prairie animals. One prairie animal, though, helps some of these plants grow! Bees feed on **nectar** from flowers. Then, the bees **pollinate**. Pollination allows the flowers to make seeds, which grow into new flowers.

Some prairie grasses change from green to gold, like the grasses shown here. The grasses change color during the fall season or because of dry weather.

Wet, Dry, Warm, and Cool

The **climate** changes as you move across America's Great Plains. The climate is wet on the eastern prairies while the western prairies are drier. On the southern prairies, the climate is warm. The northern prairies are cooler. Winters can be cold and snowy, and summers are often hot and dry.

Prairie animals have gotten used to this climate, though. Red foxes, for example, have fur that keeps them warm. Red foxes can live out in the open, but they sometimes take over dens left by other prairie animals, such as prairie dogs.

Habitat Facts

When the weather is hot and dry, fires can easily spread across a prairie. Although fire is dangerous, it is good for the soil. Animals can then eat the plants that grow well in the rich soil.

Here you can see a red fox walking over snow. Red foxes have fur that keeps them warm, and they also use their bushy tails to cover themselves up.

Burrows and Mounds

Prairie dogs are **mammals** that live in underground tunnels, called burrows. When a prairie dog digs its burrow, it leaves a mound of dirt outside. The prairie dog can then use the mound to watch out for other animals. A group of burrows is called a town. Prairie dogs from the same town playfully greet each other, but they will chase away those from other towns.

Some people think prairie dogs are pests because they dig up crops. Others think prairie dogs are important because their burrows help mix up soil and keep the ground healthy.

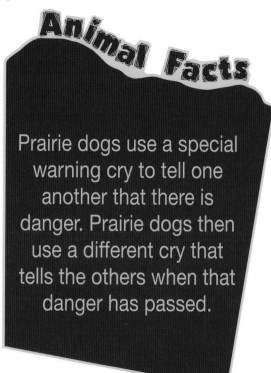

Animal Facts

Prairie dogs use a special warning cry to tell one another that there is danger. Prairie dogs then use a different cry that tells the others when that danger has passed.

This prairie dog family is sitting outside its burrow. The prairie dogs in a family work together. They share food, and they even clean one another!

Horns All Around

Have you ever seen a bison? This huge, **horned** mammal is sometimes mistakenly called a buffalo. Bison used to live throughout America's prairies. Today, bison live only in the northern prairies, where they feed on grasses and other plants.

Pronghorn antelopes are mammals named for their forklike horns. Pronghorns eat grasses, but the grasses also help pronghorns hide from **predators** like coyotes. Pronghorns are some of the fastest animals in the world. They have a top **speed** of 53 miles per hour (85 km/h). A pronghorn's predators have a hard time keeping up with it!

Bison, like the ones shown here, are the heaviest land animals in America. They can weigh between 930 and 2,200 pounds (422–998 kg)!

Prairie Chickens

Birds can be found in America's prairies, too. A prairie chicken is a small, round bird that lives in some parts of the Great Plains. Prairie chickens are interesting. When a male prairie chicken wants to find a female to **mate** with, the male snaps its tail, spreads its feathers, and makes a lot of noise. This is called booming. It is a very funny sight!

Over the years, farms and cities have spread across the Great Plains. Sadly, the number of prairie chickens has dropped because their homes are being taken away from them.

This is a greater prairie chicken, which is larger than a lesser prairie chicken. Greater prairie chickens also have darker coloring.

Grass Jumpers

Bugs are also a part of a prairie habitat. Grasshoppers are green or brown bugs that can be seen jumping through the prairie grasses. You may also hear grasshoppers singing at night.

A grasshopper has long back legs that allow the grasshopper to jump 20 times the length of its body. Imagine if you could jump 80 feet (24 m)! A male grasshopper sings when it wants to mate with a female. This sound is made when the male grasshopper rubs one of its wings against another wing or over a back leg.

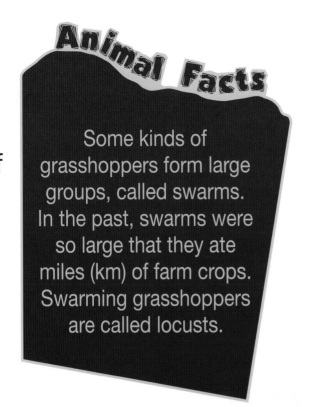

Animal Facts

Some kinds of grasshoppers form large groups, called swarms. In the past, swarms were so large that they ate miles (km) of farm crops. Swarming grasshoppers are called locusts.

This grasshopper is sitting on a blade of grass. Grasshoppers eat grass and other plants, so prairies are excellent places for them to live!

Turtles in the Grass

Ornate box turtles are cool-looking **reptiles** that can be found in a prairie habitat. "Ornate" means "fancy," and these turtles have fancy shells. Each part, or scute, of the ornate box turtle's shell has yellow lines on it. Male ornate box turtles have red or orange spots on their legs. They also have red or orange eyes.

Like all reptiles, ornate box turtles are cold blooded. This means that these turtles have body heat that changes with the heat around them. This is why ornate box turtles can often be seen warming themselves up in the morning sun.

After warming itself up in the morning, an ornate box turtle will then look for food. Ornate box turtles eat bugs, worms, and berries.

A Hop and a Puff

Great Plains toads are **amphibians** that live near bodies of water throughout a prairie habitat. Amphibians are cold blooded, and these toads spend the cold parts of the year deep inside burrows to stay warm. Great Plains toads dig these burrows using their strong back legs, which they also use for jumping.

Great Plains toads eat bugs, such as moths and flies. These toads are important to farmers because they eat many of the bugs that hurt farmers' crops. Snakes and raccoons are a toad's predators. To scare predators away, Great Plains toads will puff themselves up to look bigger!

When a male Great Plains toad wants to mate, it will call out to female toads. Calling causes the male's vocal sac, shown here, to stick out from the toad's body.

Keeping Prairies Safe

Many animals live in America's prairie habitat, but the size of the habitat is becoming smaller. Many prairies have been turned into farmland because their soil is good for growing crops. Towns and cities are also being built on prairies. These things push prairie animals out of their habitat.

People, though, are working to save the prairie habitat and the animals that live in it by setting up places where plants and animals can live freely. This means it will be possible for us to learn more about prairie animals and continue to enjoy them for a long time!

Glossary

amphibians (am-FIH-bee-unz) Animals that spend the first part of their lives in water and the rest on land.

climate (KLY-mit) The kind of weather a certain place has.

habitat (HA-beh-tat) The kind of land where animals or plants naturally live.

horned (HORND) Having a hard part on an animal's head.

mammals (MA-mulz) Animals that have a backbone, breathe air, and feed milk to their young.

mate (MAYT) When male and female animals come together to make babies.

nectar (NEK-tur) A sweet matter found in flowers.

pollinate (PAH-luh-nayt) To move pollen around to different flowers.

prairie (PRER-ee) A large place with flat land and grass but few or no trees.

predators (PREH-duh-terz) Animals that kill other animals for food.

reptiles (REP-tylz) Animals that have thin, dry pieces of skin, called scales.

speed (SPEED) How quickly something moves.

Index

Web Sites

Due to the changing nature of Internet links, PowerKids Press has developed an online list of Web sites related to the subject of this book. This site is updated regularly. Please use this link to access the list:

www.powerkidslinks.com/amhab/prairie/